The Greatest Lawyer Jokes of All Time

A Collection of Humor about Attorneys and the Legal Profession

The Greatest Lawyer Jokes of All Time

A Collection of Humor about Attorneys and the Legal Profession

William L. Pfeifer, Jr.

Pipers Willow, Inc.
www.PipersWillow.com

The Greatest Lawyer Jokes of All Time

A Collection of Humor about Attorneys and the Legal Profession

William L. Pfeifer, Jr.

Published by:
Pipers Willow, Inc.
Sheridan, Wyoming

ISBN: 0-9787277-7-0

ISBN13: 978-0-9787277-7-2

Library of Congress Control Number: 2007932245

Edited by G. Ray Kolb, Jr.

Cover Design and Typeset by Jaspal S. Bisht. For more information, contact Aruna Enterprises by email at jpl@rediffmail.com

Printed in the United States of America.

For more information, contact Pipers Willow, Inc.
by email at piperswillow@gmail.com

TABLE OF CONTENTS

Preface	vii
Dead Lawyer Jokes	1
Greedy Lawyers	17
Criminal Lawyers	41
Legal Ethics	61
The Love of Lawyers	81
Stupid Lawyers	99
Lawyers Joke About Everyone Else	109
Legalese	123
Quotable Quotes About Lawyers	131

DEDICATION

To the honest lawyers of the world.

May they rest in peace.

PREFACE

Lawyers know more lawyer jokes than anyone else. It seems that every client, every business contact, and especially every relative loves the opportunity to tell a lawyer joke to the lawyers in their lives. Some lawyers who are a little too full of themselves will get angry and insulted, but most lawyers are able to enjoy a good laugh at their own expense.

This book is the result of years of listening to lawyer jokes and never getting tired of them. Over the course of many years of practicing law, I have heard more lawyer jokes than would ever fit into one book. This book does not contain all the lawyer jokes in the world, but it does contain many of my favorites. If you are easily offended, or if you are a lawyer without a sense of humor, do not read this book. Some of the jokes are not meant for tender ears. But if you love to laugh at lawyers, or you are a lawyer who can laugh at your own profession, you will enjoy the pages that follow.

And, of course, "No representation is made that the quality of the lawyer jokes provided is greater than the quality of lawyer jokes provided by other attorneys."

The Greatest Lawyer Jokes of All Time

A Collection of Humor about Attorneys and the Legal Profession

By William L. Pfeifer, Jr.

Dead Lawyer Jokes

A lawyer awoke from surgery, and discovered that the nurse was closing the blinds by the bed. "It is dark in here," the lawyer said. "Why are you drawing the blinds?" The nurse replied, "Oh, there's a big fire across the street. We didn't want you to wake up and think the surgery was a failure."

Q: What is the definition of mixed emotions?

A: Watching an attorney drive off a cliff in your new car.

The newspaper incorrectly reported in the obituaries that an attorney named Johnson had died. The attorney, afraid of the loss of business if his clients thought he was dead, called the newspaper and angrily demanded a retraction. He threatened to file a lawsuit if the retraction was not in the next morning's newspaper.

The next morning, he opened the newspaper, and read, "We regret that the reporting of the death of Attorney Johnson was in error."

Q: How do you save a drowning lawyer?

A: Take your foot off of his head.

Dead Lawyer Jokes

Q: What do you throw to a drowning lawyer?

A: His partners.

The lawyer died, and was met by St. Peter at the gates of Heaven. Confused, the lawyer asked St. Peter, "How could I be dead? I'm a young man. I'm only 37."

St. Peter opened the lawyer's file, and disagreed. "I'm sorry sir," St. Peter replied, "but according to your billing records, you are 105."

A couple was driving to a church to get married, but on the way they were in an accident and died. They found themselves standing in front of St. Peter at the pearly gates to Heaven. They explained to St. Peter that it would not seem like Heaven to them unless they were married, and asked for permission to get married first. St. Peter thought for a moment, and then said he would see what he could do.

A few months passed by, and the couple went to see St. Peter again to ask if he had arranged their marriage. St. Peter replied that he was still working on it, and asked them to check back with him later.

A few more months went by, and when they confronted St. Peter about it, he again told them he was working on it and to check back later. This went on for five years, until St. Peter contacted them with the news that the wedding ceremony had been arranged.

The couple was ecstatic, and entered into a happy marriage for a while. But after a few years, the couple decided their marriage was not working out, and they worked up the courage to ask St. Peter if he can arrange for them to get a divorce.

The couple found St. Peter, told him the situation, and asked him if they could get a divorce. St. Peter turned red in the face with anger, and snapped at them, "A divorce? Are you kidding? It took me five years to find a priest up here. How long do you think it will take for me to find a lawyer?"

Q: What is the difference between a lawyer and a pothole?

A: People swerve to avoid potholes.

Q: What do you call a dozen attorneys skydiving?

A: Skeet.

Q: What do lawyers do when they die?

A: They lie still.

Q: What is black and brown and looks good on an attorney?

A: A Doberman pinscher.

Q: How do you get a lawyer down from a tree?

A: Cut the rope from around his neck.

Dead Lawyer Jokes

Q: What is the difference between a dead dog in the road and a dead lawyer in the road?

A: There are skid marks in front of the dog.

Q: What do you have when you have a lawyer up to his neck in concrete?

A: Not enough concrete.

Q: What is the difference between a lawyer and a trampoline?

A: You take off your shoes before jumping on a trampoline.

Q: Why won't sharks eat lawyers?

A: Professional courtesy.

Q: Why won't vultures eat lawyers?

A: There are some things that even a vulture can't eat.

Q: How can you tell if a lawyer is well hung?

A: You can't get a finger between the rope and his neck.

Q: If you were stranded on a desert island with Adolph Hitler, Saddam Hussein, and a lawyer, and you had a gun with only two bullets, what would you do?

A: Shoot the lawyer twice.

A man was walking along a lonely beach when he found a beautiful bottle. He rubbed the bottle, and suddenly a genie appeared before him. "You have freed me from the bottle," the genie said. "I will grant you three wishes. But, there is a catch. Every time you make a wish, every lawyer in the world will receive double the wish you have been granted." The man grinned, and said, "That's no problem. I'll agree to that." The genie then said, "What is your first wish?" The man replied,

"I've always wanted to own a shiny black Rolls Royce." Suddenly, a shiny black Rolls Royce appeared before the man. "Now, every lawyer in the world has two shiny black Rolls Royces. What is your second wish?" The man didn't even pause before saying, "I want one hundred million dollars in a Swiss bank account!" Suddenly, a small card appeared in his hand bearing the account number and code of his bank account. "Now, you have one hundred million dollars safely stashed in your Swiss bank account, and every lawyer in the world has two hundred million dollars hidden in Swiss bank accounts of their own. What is your final wish?" The man thought about his final wish for a few minutes, and then said, "You know, I've always wanted to donate a kidney."

Dead Lawyer Jokes

Q: Where can you find a good lawyer?

A: Six feet under the ground.

Q: How are an apple and a lawyer alike?

A: They both look good hanging from a tree.

Q: Why do they bury lawyers ten feet down instead of the six feet used for everyone else?

A: Because deep down they're not such bad people.

A man died and was sent to Hell. Upon arriving, he was informed that each person there received a customized punishment plan. As they were walking down the hallway to his room, they passed a room where a lawyer was having sex with a beautiful woman. "How is that fair?" the man complained. "I have to spend eternity being tortured, and that lawyer gets to spend it enjoying that beautiful woman." "Shut up," the demon said. "Who are you to question how that woman is punished?"

Q: Did you hear about the terrorists who held a courtroom full of lawyers hostage?

A: They threatened to release one every hour until their demands were met.

A man sat down in a restaurant with a tiger on a leash. He asked the waitress, "Do you serve lawyers here?" The waitress smiled and replied, "Well, of course we do." "Great," said the man. "I'll have the roast duck, and my tiger will have the lawyer."

Q: What do dinosaurs and honest lawyers have in common?

A: They are both extinct.

Q: What do you do if you run over a lawyer?

A: Back over him to make sure he is dead. Then, carve another notch on the steering wheel.

Q: What happens to a lawyer who jumps out of a plane at 20,000 feet without a parachute?

A: Who cares?

An attorney telephoned the governor late at night, insisting that he had to speak to him privately about an urgent and important matter. The staff reluctantly agreed to wake up the governor to take the call.

"What is so important that you need to wake me up in the middle of the night?" the governor asked.

"Judge Matherson just died," the attorney replied, "and I want to take his place."

The governor replied, "Well, if it is okay with the undertaker then it's okay with me."

Greedy Lawyers

Talk is cheap . . . until you hire a lawyer.

Q: What can a goose do, that a duck can't do, and a lawyer should do?

A: Stick his bill up his ass.

Two lawyers are in a bank when robbers burst in. While several of the robbers take the money from the tellers and from the safe, others line up the customers against a wall and start taking their wallets, purses, jewelry, etc. While waiting for the robbers to reach them, the first lawyer slips something into the second lawyer's hand. Without looking down, the second lawyer whispers, "What is this?" The first lawyer whispers back, "That's the $50 I owe you."

Sign outside of a lawyer's office: "Reasonable doubt for a reasonable price."

Q: What do you call a lawyer who doesn't chase ambulances?

A: Retired.

Greedy Lawyers

A woman approached a lawyer in a bar. She looked at him seductively, and said, "For $100, I'll do absolutely anything you want."

The lawyer reached into his wallet, handed the woman a crisp $100 bill, and said, "Here, go paint my house."

When the client couldn't understand the fee contract, the lawyer decided to simplify it for him. "Basically, if I lose I get nothing. If I win, you get nothing."

An architect, a doctor, and a lawyer were arguing over who had the smartest dog. They decided to have a contest to settle the issue by having their dogs perform their best trick.

The architect said to his dog, "Show them the tower we visited last summer." The dog ran over to the table and build a model of the Eifel Tower out of toothpicks. The architect tossed him a cookie as his reward.

"Impressive," said the doctor, "but watch this. Show 'em, Sam." The doctor's dog ran to the table and performed an emergency Caesarian on a cow. A few minutes later, both the cow and her baby were doing great. The doctor also gave his dog a cookie for a reward.

The lawyer smiled, and nodded to his dog. The lawyer's dog ran over, screwed the other two dogs, took their cookies, and went out to lunch.

Greedy Lawyers

After describing his legal problem to the lawyer, the client asked how much the lawyer would charge to represent him. The lawyer thought for a moment, and then said, "Well, I have good news and bad news."

Eager to hear something good about his situation, the client asked, "Well, what is the good news?"

The lawyer replied, "My son was just accepted to Harvard Law School."

The client, unsure what this had to do with his case, congratulated the lawyer and asked, "So what is the bad news?"

"The bad news," the lawyer replied, "is that you are going to pay for it."

Q: What is the difference between a lawyer and a herd of buffalo?

A: A lawyer charges more.

A reporter saw a man standing outside a courtroom wearing nothing but a wooden barrel. "Oh, I guess you must have lost your case," the reporter said.

The man answered, "No, we won."

A lawyer reached the point in the client interview where it was time to talk about his fee schedule.

"Okay," the lawyer said as he handed the contract to the client. "You owe me

$2500 down and $527.38 per month for the next thirty-six months."

"That sounds like a car payment schedule," the client replied.

"You're exactly right," the lawyer said. "It's mine."

A new client had just come in to see a lawyer. "Can you tell me how much you charge?" asked the client.

"Of course", the lawyer replied, "I charge $200 to answer three questions!"

"Well that's a bit steep, isn't it?"

"Yes it is", said the lawyer, "but that is my fee. And what's your third question?"

Q: How was the lawyer injured in a car accident?

A: The ambulance stopped too quickly.

An attorney had to hire a plumber to make repairs to his home. The plumber quickly discovered and repaired the problem, and presented the lawyer with a bill for $750.00

"$750.00??! For less than an hour's work? Why, I'm an attorney and I don't make that kind of income," the lawyer complained.

"I know," replied the plumber. "When I was a lawyer, I didn't make that kind of income either."

The day after a verdict had been entered against his client, the lawyer rushed to the judge's chambers, demanding that the case be reopened, saying: "I have new evidence that makes a huge difference in my client's defense."

The judge asked, "What new evidence could you possibly have now?"

The lawyer replied, "My client has an extra $10,000, and I just found out about it!"

Q: What is the difference between a lawyer and a street hooker?

A: There are some things a hooker won't do for money.

The two partners in a law firm were having lunch one day when one of them jumped up and said, "I have to go back to the office. I forgot to lock the safe!"

"What are you worried about," the other lawyer replied. "We're both here."

A barber gave a haircut to the young Baptist minister at the new church. When the minister tried to pay for the haircut, the barber refused to accept the money, saying "you do God's work." The next morning, a box of Bibles was delivered to his shop.

A policeman came into the barber shop for a haircut. When he tried to pay, the barber refused payment from him as well, saying "you protect the public." The next morning, the barber found a box of a dozen doughnuts at the door to his shop.

A lawyer came in for a haircut, and the barber refused payment from him, saying "you serve the justice system." The next morning the barber found a dozen lawyers waiting for a free haircut.

Q: How do you know it is a cold day outside?

A: When you see lawyers putting their hands in their own pockets.

A passenger plane was having engine trouble, and the pilot instructed the crew to have the passengers take their seats to prepare for an emergency landing. A few minutes later, the pilot asked the crew if everyone was buckled in and ready.

"We're almost ready," one of the staff replied. "Everyone is seated except the lawyers. They haven't finished passing out business cards yet."

A lawyer was working late in his office one night when the Devil appeared to him. The Devil told the lawyer that the lawyer could get clients to pay him huge legal fees, win every time he went to court, stop having to work hard, be able to seduce any woman, and live a long and prosperous life.

"In exchange for all of this," the Devil stated, "all I want is your soul and the souls of your children."

The lawyer sat back in his chair, rubbed his chin, and pondered the Devil's offer. Finally, he leaned forward and asked, "So, what's the catch?"

Q: What did the trial lawyer name his daughter?

A: Sue.

A doctor and a lawyer were attending a cocktail party when the doctor was approached by a man who asked advice on how to handle a medical situation.

The doctor mumbled some generic medical advice, then turned to the lawyer and asked, "How do you handle the situation when you are asked for advice during a social function?"

"Just send him a invoice for your advice, and he'll get the point," replied the lawyer.

The next morning, the doctor arrived at his office and issued the man a $50 invoice. That afternoon he received a $100 invoice from the lawyer.

A lawyer was driving down a curvy road in his new Mercedes thinking about all of the money he had won that day in court. Not paying attention to his driving, he ran off of the road and hit a tree.

Battered, cut, and bruised, he crawled out of the car crying, "My Mercedes! My Mercedes!"

The ambulance arrived, and the paramedics were lifting the attorney into the ambulance when the lawyer noticed that his left arm was gone. The lawyer then started screaming, "My Rolex! My Rolex!"

Q. What's the difference between a good lawyer and a bad lawyer?

A. A bad lawyer can let a case drag out for several years. A good lawyer can make it last even longer.

NASA was interviewing people from various professions to go on a mission to Mars. Only one could go, and could never return to Earth.

The first applicant was an engineer. The NASA interviewer asked the engineer how much he wanted to be paid to go to Mars. "One million dollars," the engineer answered, "and I want the money donated to my alma mater, M.I.T."

The second applicant was a doctor, and the NASA interviewer asked him the same question. "I want two million dollars," the doctor answered. "I want one million of it given to my family to take care of them when I am gone, and one million to go to the Shriner's Hospitals to help crippled children."

The final applicant was a lawyer. When asked how much money he wanted, he told the interviewer he wanted three million dollars.

"Why should we pay you so much more than the other applicants?" the interviewer asked.

The lawyer slid his chair up close to the interviewer, and whispered in his ear. "If you give me three million, I'll give you one million, I'll keep one million, and we'll send the engineer to Mars."

A couple of lawyers are sitting in a bar having a drink when a gorgeous blonde walks into the room. One of the lawyers says, "God, I'd love to screw her!"

The other lawyer looks puzzled, and turns to him and asks, "Out of what?"

Lawyer bumper sticker: "Hit me — I'm a lawyer."

A golfer hooked his tee shot over a hill and onto the next fairway. Walking toward his ball, he saw a man lying on the ground, groaning with pain.

"I'm an attorney," the man said," and this is going to cost you $5000 if you don't want me taking you to court."

"I'm sorry, I'm really sorry," the concerned golfer replied. "But I did yell 'fore'."

"I'll take it," the attorney said.

Greedy Lawyers

Q: How many lawyers does it take to change a light bulb?

A: Three: one to climb the ladder and turn the bulb, one to shake him off of the ladder, and one to sue the ladder manufacturer.

A Mexican thief liked to slip across the border and rob banks in Texas. He managed to steal so much money that a reward was offered for his capture, dead or alive. A rugged bounty hunter decided that he would track him down, steal the loot from the thief, and then take the thief back for the reward too.

After a lengthy search, he traced the thief to his favorite bar, snuck up behind him, put a gun to the thief's head, and said, "Okay scumbag, you're mine now. Tell me where the money is, and I'll let you live. If you don't tell me, I'll put a bullet through your brain."

Unfortunately, the thief didn't speak English, and the bounty hunter didn't speak Spanish. However, a bilingual lawyer was sitting at a nearby table, and offered to serve as the translator. The lawyer translated the message to the Mexican, and the terrified thief admitted that the money was buried beneath the old oak tree behind the church.

"What did he say?" asked the bounty hunter.

The lawyer answered, "He said 'Go to hell, you greasy gringo bastard. You don't have the balls to shoot me.'"

Greedy Lawyers

A dog ran into a butcher shop and grabbed a roast off the counter. The butcher recognized the dog as belonging to a lawyer with an office down the street.

Angry over the animal's behavior, the butcher called the lawyer and asked, "If your dog stole a roast from my butcher shop, would you be liable for the cost of the meat?"

The lawyer replied, "That's absolutely correct. How much was the roast?"

"$8.95," the butcher answered.

A few days later the butcher received an invoice from the lawyer's office that read: "Legal consultation: $150. Credit to account: $8.95. Balance due to attorney: $141.05."

A fundraiser for a local charity noticed that the most successful lawyer in town had not made a contribution to their fund drive. Everyone knew the lawyer made several million dollars a year, so the fundraiser decided to give him a call.

"Sir, according to our records you have not contributed anything towards supporting our charitable causes in the community. Could you make a donation to help the needy today?"

The lawyer angrily replied, "A donation? Sir, were you aware that my elderly mother requires around-the-clock nursing care just to stay alive?!"

The fundraiser, starting to understand the situation, felt embarrassed and began to stammer, "Well, no sir, I'm . . ."

The lawyer interrupted. "And were you aware that my sister's husband was killed in a car accident, that she is in a wheelchair, and she has three kids to support on her own?!"

The worker felt completely ashamed, and again tried to speak. "I'm terribly sorry sir, I . . ."

"And were you aware that my own brother is a missionary in Rwanda, bringing food and hope to the suffering people there?"

The fundraiser, feeling completely humiliated at this point, again tried to make his apology. "Sir, I am so sorry sir, please . . . "

"The gall of you people!" the lawyer interrupted again. "I don't give a dime of my money to them, so what makes you think I would give it to you!"

The dying lawyer was desperate to take his life's savings with him when he died. He instructed his wife to withdraw all of his savings from the bank, put the money in his briefcase, and put the briefcase in the attic directly over his bed. His plan was that at the moment he died, he would grab the briefcase on his way to Heaven.

After his death, his wife went to the attic to see if the lawyer's plan had worked. She saw that the briefcase was sitting where she left it, with all of the money still inside.

"Stupid old man," the wife said to herself. "I told him we should have put the money in the basement."

Criminal Lawyers & Criminals

The defendant sat down next to his attorney in the courtroom at the start of his trial, and whispered to his lawyer, "I'm so nervous! I've never been in a courtroom before."

The lawyer whispered back, "I know how you feel. This is my first time in court too."

When a person assists a criminal in breaking the law before he gets arrested, the person is called an accomplice. When a person assists a criminal in breaking the law after he gets arrested, the person is called a criminal defense lawyer.

A farmer was arrested on a charge of bestiality, and went to a retired judge for advice on choosing a lawyer to represent him. The retired judge told the farmer, "I know a great trial lawyer who puts on a great show in the courtroom, but he is expensive and is not very good at choosing a jury."

The farmer said, "Well, I know this is important, but I don't have much money and probably can't afford an expensive lawyer."

"Well," the retired judge replied, "there is another lawyer who doesn't look like much and isn't that great in the courtroom, but he is cheap and he can pick a jury better than any lawyer I've ever seen."

The farmer decided to hire the cheap lawyer and hoped he would pick a good jury, but he was worried when he heard the witness testify, " I saw Dwight mount his goat from behind doggie style, or I guess I mean goat style, and when he finished the goat turned around and licked Dwight's little prick too."

The farmer turned red in the face and was about to faint in his seat, when he overheard a juror in overalls whisper to the juror next to him, "A good goat will do that, you know."

A man was arrested for drunk driving, and was taken before the judge for trial. The judge leaned over the bench and asked the man, "Do you know the penalty for drunk driving in this state?"

The man looked back up at the judge and replied, "I don't know; is it re-election to the Senate?"

The judge looked at the defendant in his court and said, "Due to the seriousness of your case, I'm going to give you three lawyers."

"Forget the lawyers," the defendant replied. "Just give me one good witness."

The judge scowled over the bench at the defendant and said, "Potter, I can't believe you've gotten another arrest. Didn't I tell you I never wanted to see you in my courtroom again?"

"That's what I tried to tell the officer," the man replied, "but he just wouldn't listen."

After the judge sentenced the defendant, he asked the defendant if he had anything further to say.

"Well, while we are here, you may as well add a few more years to my sentence."

The judge was puzzled by this statement and asked the defendant, "Why would you want me to do that?"

"Oh, it isn't that I want you to add more time to my sentence," the defendant replied, "but I'm about to beat the shit out of my worthless lawyer, so I figured we could take care of my sentencing for that while I'm here."

The lawyer discovered a bag of pot in his son's sock drawer. When his son returned from school, he confronted him with the evidence.

"Dad, I swear I'm innocent," the lawyer's son claimed. "It is just like your criminal trials; the evidence must have been planted by a crooked cop."

An attorney got home late one evening after spending a very exhausting day trying to get a stay of execution for a client, James Wright, who was due to be hanged for murder at midnight. His last minute plea for clemency to the governor had failed, and the lawyer was tired and depressed.

As soon as he walked through the front door, his wife started nagging him about how late it was, where had he been, had he been drinking, etc. Too worn out to argue, he went and poured himself a glass of bourbon and headed off for a hot shower while his wife's tirade continued in the background.

While he was in the shower, the phone rang. The wife answered and was told that the governor changed his mind at the last minute and had granted the stay of execution.

Finally realizing what a day he must have had, the wife decided to go upstairs to give him the good news. As she opened the bathroom door, she was greeted by the sight of her husband's rear end as he was bent over naked drying his legs and feet.

"They're not hanging Wright tonight," she said.

The lawyer whirled around and screamed, "FOR CRYING OUT LOUD, WOMAN, DON'T YOU EVER LET UP??!!"

Q: What is a criminal lawyer?

A: Redundant.

In a murder trial, the criminal defense lawyer was cross examining the coroner:

Attorney: Before you signed the death certificate, did you take his pulse?

Coroner: No.

Attorney: Did you listen to his heart?

Coroner: No.

Attorney: Did you check his breathing?

Coroner: No.

Attorney: So, since you didn't even check his vital signs, you can't even be sure that this man is dead, can you?

Coroner: Well, his brain is sitting in a jar on my desk, but I supose he could be out practicing law somewhere.

"How can I ever thank you?" the woman said to her lawyer, after hearing the not guilty verdict.

"Ms. Duncan," the lawyer replied," ever since the Phoenicians invented money there has been only one answer to that question."

After the jury found the lawyer's client not guilty, the lawyer's curiosity got the better of him. "So now that it is over, tell me the truth. Did you break into those houses?"

"Well, after hearing what you said in court today, I'm starting to think it wasn't me."

Q: What is the punishment for bigamy?

A: Two mothers-in-law.

A man accused of a crime walks into the lobby of the large law firm, and asked the receptionist, "Do you have any criminal attorneys?" The receptionist smiled and said, "Well of course, but the cops can't prove it!"

The Lawyer's Creed: All men are innocent until proven broke.

At the height of the trial, the prosecuting attorney was attacking a crucial defense witness. "Isn't it true," the prosecutor asked, "that you accepted a bribe of $10,000 to compromise this case?"

The witness stared into space, as if he had not heard the question.

"Sir," the prosecutor repeated, "isn't it true that you accepted $10,000 to compromise this case?"

The witness yawned, and still did not reply.

Finally, the judge leaned over to the witness and said, "Mr. Watkins, please answer the question."

"Oh, I apologize," the witness replied, "I thought he was talking to you."

The defendant told the lawyer the story of his arrest, of being caught red-handed, the seven witnesses to the crime, and his own confession. The defendant told the lawyer: "I know the case against me is really strong, but I have eighty thousand dollars in my bank account to spend on my defense." Choosing his words carefully, the lawyer smiled and told the defendant: "Well, hire me, and I promise you that you will not go to prison with that amount of money in your bank account."

The lawyer came home late, and apologized to his wife for being late for dinner. "Sorry," he said, "but I was at the jail interviewing a client. He wants to use the SODDI defense."

"Do you mean self-defense?"

"No," the lawyer explained, "the SODDI defense—Some Other Dude Did It."

The small-town prosecuting attorney called his first witness, an elderly woman, to the stand. He approached her and asked, "Mrs. Walker, do you know me?"

She responded, "Why, yes, I do know you, Mr. Doggett. I've known you since you were a young boy, and frankly, you've been a big disappointment to me. You lie, you cheat on your wife, you manipulate people and talk about them behind their backs. You think you're a big shot when you haven't the brains to realize you never will amount to anything more than a two-bit paper pusher. Yes, I know you."

The lawyer was stunned. Not knowing what else to do, he pointed across the room and asked, "Mrs. Walker, do you know the defense attorney?"

She again replied, "Why, yes, I do. I've known Mr. Duncan since he was a youngster, too. He's lazy, bigoted, and he has a drinking problem. He can't build a normal relationship with anyone and his law practice is one of the worst in the entire state. Not to mention he cheated on his wife with three different women. One of them was your wife. Yes, I know him."

The defense attorney turned completely red in the face and thought he was going to faint. At that point, the judge called a recess of the proceedings and asked both counselors to approach the bench. In a quiet and threatening voice, the judge said, "If either of you bastards asks her if she knows me, I'll throw your sorry asses in jail for contempt."

Q: What's the difference between O. J. Simpson and Pee-Wee Herman?

A: It only took twelve jerks to get O.J. off.

Slogan on a lawyer's coffee cup: "It's not illegal; just undocumented."

The jail inmate sat down in the conference room to meet with his attorney. "Mr. Cheatam," the inmate pleaded, "you've got to get me out of this!"

"Mr. Dumas," the lawyer replied, "there's no need to worry, I've got everything under control. If I can't prove that you were out of town when the murder occurred, then I'll have a psychiatrist testify that you were temporarily insane. If that doesn't work, I'll pay one of the prosecutor's witnesses to forget what he witnessed. Plus, I'm playing golf with the judge on Sunday, and a couple of the jurors are poker buddies of mine."

"That's great news," the inmate replied. "Is there anything I should do before trial?"

"Yes," the lawyer replied. "Try to escape."

A law student went to the most successful criminal defense lawyer in town, and asked him what was the most important thing he needed to know to practice criminal law.

"That's simple, my boy," the lawyer replied. "Just remember that all men are innocent until proven indigent."

As the defendant's murder trial was drawing to a close, the defendant was worried that he would be convicted. "What will they do to me if we lose?" the defendant asked his lawyer.

"They'll probably execute you," the lawyer replied. "Around here, they do the executions by hanging."

"Hanging!" the man exclaimed. "But if they hang me, who will support my family?"

"Don't worry," the lawyer stated in a calm tone of voice. "I've got everything under control."

The defendant sighed with relief. "Good, I'm glad you've got a plan to prove my innocence."

The lawyer chuckled. "No, I don't have a plan to prove your innocence, but after they hang you I'm going to sue them for whiplash!"

Legal Ethics

After hearing the client's story, the lawyer began to speak. "Well," the lawyer said, "if you really want my honest opinion . . . "

"I don't," the client interrupted. "I want your professional advice."

Q: Why did God make snakes before lawyers?

A: Practice.

One afternoon, a wealthy lawyer was riding in his shiny limousine when he saw two men along the roadside eating grass. Disturbed, he ordered his driver to stop, and he got out to investigate the situation.

He walked up to the men and asked, "Why are you eating grass?"

"We don't have any money for food," one of the men replied. "We have to eat grass or we will starve to death."

The lawyer looked at the men with tears in his eyes, and said, "Come with me to my house, and I will feed you."

"Kind sir," one of the men said, "we also have our wives and children with us. They are over there, sitting under that tree."

"Bring them too," the lawyer said.

All of the people jammed into the limousine to start the drive to the lawyer's house. One of the men turned to the lawyer and said, "You are being so good to us. Thank you for taking us with you."

"Glad to do it," the lawyer said. "You'll love my place. I fired the gardener last month, and the grass is almost a foot high!"

Q: How does an attorney sleep?

A: First he lies on one side, then he lies on the other.

Lawyer t-shirt: "Trust me—I'm a lawyer."

A lawyer walked into the offices of the local newspaper and said that he wanted to place a classified ad.

"What would you like it to say?" asked the ad salesman.

"$5,000 cash reward for the return of wife's brown tabby cat. No questions asked," said the lawyer.

"I'm impressed that you would do that for your wife, but don't you think the reward is a little excessive?" asked the salesman.

"Nah," said the lawyer. "I drowned the damn thing a week ago."

Q: What do you call a lawyer gone bad?

A: Senator.

Legal Ethics

The senior partner of the law firm was walking through the parking lot with two of his associates when they found an old oil lamp. Out of curiosity, they rubbed the lamp, and suddenly a genie appeared.

The genie said that he usually granted three wishes to whomever released him from the lamp, but since there were three of them he would give each of them one wish.

The first associate said, "I want to be on the beach, surrounded with beautiful women." And in a puff of smoke, the first associate disappeared.

The second associate said, "I want to be on a cruise ship sailing around the world." And in another puff of smoke, the second associate disappeared.

Turning to the senior partner, the genie asked him for his wish.

The senior partner answered, "I want those two back in the office now!"

Q: What is the difference between a liar and a lawyer?

A: The pronunciation.

The lawyer's wife was complaining about the condition of their house. She said, "Look at this place! Our furniture is old, the shingles are coming off the roof, the shutters are falling off, and the carpet is worn thin. This place needs to be completely remodeled."

"Don't worry," the lawyer replied. "Mr. Harris just hired me to handle his divorce, and he is filthy rich. As soon as I finish breaking up their home, I can fix up ours."

Q: Why is arguing with a lawyer like mud wrestling with a pig?

A: After a while, you realize the pig actually enjoys it.

An attorney charged his client $1000 in cash for legal services. After the man left, the attorney discovered that the man had actually paid him $1100 by mistake. The lawyer spent the rest of the afternoon struggling with his ethical dilemma: should he tell his partner?

A group of lawyers went deer hunting and paired off in twos for the day. That night, one of the lawyers returned to the campsite alone, staggering under the weight of an eight-point buck.

When the other lawyers saw he was alone, one of them asked, "Where's Charlie?"

The lawyer replied, "Charlie had a stroke of some kind. He's a couple of miles back up the road."

'You left Charlie laying out there and carried the deer back?"

The lawyer answered, "Yep, it was a tough decision. But as I figure it, no one is going to steal Charlie."

In a courtroom, everyone swears to tell the truth—except the lawyers.

Q: What do lawyers and sperm have in common?

A: It takes 300,000 of them to make one human being.

A good lawyer knows the law. A great lawyer knows the judge.

The young reporter was excited to receive his first big break covering the courthouse news. Since he wanted to make sure to do a good job, he went to a senior reporter for advice on how to tell when a lawyer was telling the truth and when he was lying.

"It is pretty easy if you watch the body language," the senior reporter told him. "If he touches his hair, he's telling the truth. If he scratches his nose, he's telling the truth. But if he opens his mouth and moves his lips . . . ."

Q: Why are lawyers prohibited from having sex with their clients?

A: To prevent clients from being billed twice for the same service.

Q: What are lawyers good for?

A: They make used car salesmen look good.

Legal Ethics

The lawyer walked into the courthouse, and saw the opposing counsel talking to several people in the hallway. The lawyer approached her and asked, "Are those your witnesses?"

"Yes, they are here to testify for my client today," the opposing counsel answered.

The lawyer sighed and said, "Well, I guess we'll take the settlement then. I've used those witnesses three times myself."

Q: How can you tell when a lawyer is lying?

A: His lips are moving.

A guy walked into the post office, and saw an overweight bald man in a suit standing at the counter, placing "love" stamps on a stack of pink envelopes and then spraying each envelope with perfume. The guy, being curious, approached the man and asked what he was doing.

"I'm sending out 1000 Valentine's Day cards, signed 'Guess who?'"

"But why would you do that?"

"I'm a divorce lawyer," the man answered.

An old man was on his death bed. He wanted badly to take some of his money with him. He called his priest, his doctor and his lawyer to his bedside. "Here's

$30,000 cash to be held by each of you. I trust you to put this in my coffin when I die so I can take all my money with me."

At the funeral, each man put an envelope in the coffin. Riding away in a limousine, the priest suddenly broke into tears and confessed, "I only put $20,000 into the envelope because I needed $10,000 for a new baptistery."

"Well, since we're confiding in each other," said the doctor, "I only put $10,000 in the envelope because we needed a new machine at the hospital which cost $20,000."

The lawyer was aghast. "I'm ashamed of both of you," he exclaimed. "I want it known that when I put my envelope in that coffin, it held my personal check for the full $30,000."

Q: Why do lawyers use lots of tanning oil at the beach?

A: They are used to doing all of their lying indoors.

A doctor went into a bar to try to meet women. Each time he approached a woman, she would seem interested until he said he was a doctor, at which point the woman would lose interest and walk away. After trying and failing with several women, the bartender called him over and spoke to him. "The problem," the bartender said, "is that this is a lawyer bar, and the women who come here are looking to meet lawyers." The doctor thought for a moment, then went up to another woman and introduced himself as a lawyer. Immediately she offered to buy him a drink, and shortly thereafter he was in her bedroom. "Wow, this is great," he thought as he climbed into her bed. "I've been a lawyer for less than an hour, and I'm already screwing someone."

Q: What is the difference between a lawyer and a prostitute?

A: A prostitute stops screwing you once you are dead.

Q: How many lawyers does it take to change a light bulb?

A: None, lawyers can't change light bulbs. Now, if you need to screw a light bulb. . . .

A lawyer was driving down the road in his SUV and noticed a car in the ditch. He started to drive by without stopping, but then noticed that the driver was a beautiful woman, so he decided to pull over and help her.

As he was hooking her car to the back of his SUV, he said, "You know, you are the first pregnant woman I've ever helped out of a ditch."

"But I'm not pregnant," the woman said.

"I know," the lawyer replied, "but you're not out of the ditch yet either, are you?'

Legal Ethics

Q: What do honest lawyers and UFOs have in common?

A: You always hear about them, but you never see them.

Q: How do a teacher, an accountant, and a lawyer answer the question "What is two plus two?"

Teacher Answer: "That's easy, the answer is four."

Accountant Answer: "Well, it looks like it will work out to approximately four, but let's run it through our computer spread sheet to double-check those figures."

Lawyer Answer: "What would you like the answer to be?"

Q: What is a lawyer?

A: Someone who makes sure he gets what is coming to you.

Q: What do you get when you cross a lawyer with a demon from hell?

A: Another lawyer.

The madam opened the brothel door to see a rather dignified, well-dressed good looking man in his late 40s or early 50s.

"May I help you?" she asked.

"I want to see Natalie," the man replied.

"Sir, Natalie is one of our most expensive ladies. Perhaps you would prefer someone else," said the madam.

"No. I must see Natalie," was the man's reply.

Just then, Natalie appeared and announced to the man that she charged $1,000 a visit. Without hesitation, the man pulled out ten one-hundred dollar bills, gave them to Natalie, and they went upstairs. After an hour, the man calmly left.

The next night, the same man appeared again, demanding to see Natalie. Natalie explained that no one had ever come back two nights in a row—too expensive—and there were no discounts. The price was still $1,000. Again the man pulled out the money, gave it to Natalie and they went upstairs. After an hour, he left.

The following night the man was there again. Everyone was astounded that he had come for the third consecutive night, but he paid Natalie and they went upstairs. After their session, Natalie questioned the man. "No one has ever used me three nights in a row. Where are you from?" she asked.

The man replied, "South Carolina."

"Really" she said. "I have family in South Carolina."

"I know," the man said. "Your father died and I am your sister's attorney. She asked me to give you your $3,000 inheritance."

Q: What is the difference between God and a lawyer?

A: God doesn't think he is a lawyer.

The Love of Lawyers

Q: What does it mean when a lawyer is in your bed, gasping for breath and calling your name?

A: You didn't hold the pillow down long enough.

A man escaped from a prison where he'd been locked up for 15 years. He broke into a lawyer's house to look for money, guns, and the keys to the car. Inside the house, he found a lawyer and his young beautiful wife in bed. He ordered the lawyer out of bed and tied him to a chair. While tying the lawyer's wife to the bed, the convict got on top of her, kissed her neck, then got up and went into the bathroom.

While the convict was in the bathroom, the lawyer whispered to his wife: "Listen, this guy is an escaped convict. Look at his clothes! He's probably spent a lot of time in jail and hasn't seen a woman in years. I saw how he kissed your neck. If he wants sex, don't resist, don't complain...do whatever he tells you. Satisfy him no matter how much he nauseates you. This guy is obviously very dangerous. If he gets angry, he'll kill us both. Be strong, honey. "I love you!"

His wife responded: "He wasn't kissing my neck. He was whispering in my ear. He told me that he's gay, thinks you're cute, and asked if we had any Vaseline. I told him it was in the bathroom. Be strong honey. I love you, too."

Q: What is the best thing about a blow job from a female lawyer?

A: The ten minutes of silence.

A minister woke up in a hospital bed after a terrible car accident, and saw the doctor standing by his bedside. The minister could tell from the look on the doctor's face that he was dying, and he asked the doctor, "So, tell me the truth. How long do I have left to live?"

The doctor bowed his head, and replied that he doubted the minister would live through the night.

The minister paused in thought for a moment, then said, "Call for my lawyer."

When the lawyer arrived, the minister asked for his doctor to stand on one side of the bed, and the lawyer to stand on the other side. The man then laid back and closed his eyes. After a few moments of silence, the doctor asked why he asked for them both to be there.

The minister replied "I've tried to follow Jesus's example all of my life. Jesus died with a thief on either side of him, so I thought I'd go out the same way."

A lawyer is an expert on justice in the same way a prostitute is an expert on love.

Q: What do lawyers use for birth control?

A: Their personalities.

A lawyer was talking to his son about starting college, and asked, "Now what made you decide you wanted to be a doctor instead of a lawyer?"

"Well, Dad," answered the son, "did you ever hear anybody get up in a crowd and shout frantically, 'Is there a lawyer in the house?' "

Q: What do you get when you sleep with a judge?

A: An honorable discharge.

For several years, a lawyer had been taking his annual vacation at a bed and breakfast in the mountains. During that time, he developed an infatuation with the owner's young daughter. One year, he finally succeeded in seducing her.

The next year, when he returned for his vacation, he saw the young woman holding a small baby. As he recovered from the shock of finding out he was a father, he asked the young woman, "Why didn't you tell me? I would have done the honorable thing and would have returned to marry you."

"I thought about it," the young woman replied. "I spent a long time discussing it with my parents. Ultimately, we decided it would be better to have a bastard in the family than a lawyer."

Q: What happens when a lawyer takes Viagra?

A: He grows taller.

After spending a frustrating afternoon having his deposition taken by an arrogant lawyer, the man was telling his wife about the experience over drinks at a restaurant. As he became more and more agitated recounting the events of the day, the man stood up in the restaurant and shouted, "All lawyers are assholes!"

"Hey, I resent that," a man at the other side of the restaurant yelled back. "I should come over there and kick your ass!"

"Why," the first man asked, "are you one of those damn lawyers?"

"No," the man responded, "I'm an asshole!"

Q: Why did the Post Office recall their latest line of stamps?

A: They had pictures of famous lawyers on them, and the customers could not figure out which side to spit on.

A paralegal was picked up by a man in a bar, and had a one-night stand with him without ever finding out anything about him. A couple of months later, the woman realized she was pregnant with the man's child, and went to hire a private detective to find him.

"What can you tell me about the man that might help me find him?" the detective asked.

"Well, the only thing I know for sure is that he was a lawyer," the woman replied.

"How do you know he was a lawyer?" the detective asked.

"He made me do all the work, never thanked me, and took credit for the results."

A young lawyer woke up one morning with a terrible hangover. He went into the living room, where his wife was sitting on the sofa. He said to her, "Wow, I have such a bad headache. I must have made a fool of myself at the office party last night."

"Yes, you did," his wife replied. "You were so drunk that you got into an argument with the managing partner of the firm and cussed him out."

"Well, piss on him," the young lawyer said.

"Actually, you did - and he fired you," she said.

The young lawyer became more angry, and snapped, "Well, screw that son of a bitch."

"I did," said his wife. "You go back to work on Monday."

Q: What is the difference between a cat and a lawyer?

A: One is an arrogant creature who will ignore you and treat you with contempt unless it thinks it can get something from you, and the other is a house pet.

A lawyer and his wife were on their honeymoon. The lawyer took off his pants and handed them to his new wife. "See if these fit," he said.

"Well of course they don't fit," she said, handing the pants back to him.

"That's right," the lawyer said. "So now you know who will wear the pants in our house."

The wife looked at her husband for a moment, then took off her panties. The lawyer started to smile, until she handed them to him and said, "Now you try these on and see if they fit."

"Are you kidding? I can't get into those," the lawyer said.

"That's right," his wife replied, "and you won't until you stop acting like an ass."

Q: What is wrong with lawyer jokes?

A: Lawyers don't think they are funny and nobody else thinks they are jokes.

The lawyer sat down to talk to his son about the birds and the bees. "Son," the lawyer said, "I remember the first time I had sex. In fact, I still have the receipt."

Q: What do you say to a lawyer with an IQ of 50?

A: Good morning, your Honor.

A doctor told his patient that he only had a week to live. "But, surely there must be something I can do to extend my life?" the patient begged.

"Well," the doctor said, "you could marry a lawyer, and it will feel like the longest week of your life."

Q: What is the difference between a lawyer and a bucket of pond scum?

A: The bucket.

Two old friends, one a lawyer and the other a therapist, met for lunch to chat. The lawyer said to the therapist, "You know, I don't understand, but people take an instant dislike to me when they find out I'm a lawyer. Why do you think that is?"

"Well," the old friend replied, "maybe it just saves time."

Q: How many lawyers does it take to change a light bulb?

A: None. They would rather keep their clients in the dark.

Q: Why can't lawyers go to the beach?

A: Cats keep trying to bury them in the sand.

Q: What is the difference between a female lawyer and a pit bull?

A: Lipstick.

Q: What is the difference between a lawyer and a vulture?

A: Lawyers get frequent flyer points.

Q: What do you get when you cross a lawyer with a snake?

A: Another lawyer.

Q: What is the difference between a lawyer and an onion?

A: You cry when you cut up an onion.

A lawyer and his wife entered a dentist's office, and the dentist asked, "How can I help you?"

The lawyer said, "I want a tooth pulled. I don't want pain pills or gas or Novocain or anything else because I'm in a terrible hurry. Just pull the tooth as quickly as possible."

"You're a brave man," said the dentist. "Now, show me which tooth it is."

The lawyer turns to his wife and says: "Open your mouth for the dentist, dear."

Q: What is the difference between a lawyer and a football?

A: You only get three points for kicking a football between the uprights.

Stupid Lawyers

A guy in a bar leaned over to the guy next to him and said, "Want to hear a lawyer joke?"

The guy next to him replied, "Well, before you tell that joke, you should know that I'm 6 feet tall, 200 pounds of muscle, and I'm a lawyer. And the guy sitting next to me is 6'2" tall, 225 pounds of muscle, and he's a lawyer too. Now, do you still want to tell that joke?"

The first guy says, "No, I don't want to have to explain it twice."

A man went into a brain store to get some human brains for a lab experiment. He saw a section of the store was marked as carrying a special line of brains of professionals from the community. The man questioned the owner about the price of the brains.

"How much for that jar of engineer brains?" the man asked.

"Three dollars an ounce," the owner replied.

"What about those computer programmer brains, how much are those?" the man asked.

"Five dollars an ounce."

"And how much are the lawyer brains?" the man asked.

"Those are one thousand dollars per ounce," the owner answered.

"That's crazy! Why are lawyer brains so much more expensive than everyone else's?" the man asked.

The owner replied to the man, "Do you have any idea how many lawyers we had to kill to get one ounce of brain?"

Two lawyers were chatting with each other at the bar. The first lawyer said, "Hey, I hear you are handling the Dergenberg estate. How much did that old man leave behind?"

The second lawyer got a puzzled look on his face, then replied, "Well, as far as I can tell, everything."

A lawyer and his wife were walking through a park when a pigeon flew overhead and dropped a blob of poop on the woman's head.

"EW!!" exclaimed the woman. "Quick, get some toilet paper!"

The lawyer replied, "Why? That bird is blocks away by now."

To celebrate their 20th anniversary, a lawyer and his wife returned to the hotel where they spent their honeymoon. As they went to bed, the lawyer turned to his wife and slyly said, "Honey, what were you thinking twenty years ago tonight?"

"Honestly," his wife replied, "I was thinking that I'd screw your brains out."

The lawyer grinned and asked, "So, what are you thinking now?"

His wife replied, "I guess that it worked."

A lawyer was bragging about how much smarter he was than everyone else. "Why, I just finished a puzzle, and it only took me six months to do it."

"Six months? That seems like a long time to me," said the client.

"Not for this one," the lawyer explained. "The box said eight to twelve years."

Q: Why is it so common for attorneys to get lost in thought?

A: They are in unfamiliar territory.

A lawyer was sightseeing in a historical village, and went into the old blacksmith shop. The smithy was in the middle of demonstrating how horseshoes were made, and had just placed a red-hot horseshoe on a metal table to cool. Before he could be warned, the lawyer picked up the hot horseshoe, and then instantly dropped it.

The blacksmith asked. "Did you get burned badly?"

"No," the embarrassed lawyer replied, "it just doesn't take long to look at a horseshoe."

A lawyer was driving down the road reading his text messages, and carelessly rear-ended the car in front of him. Hoping to turn the tables on the other driver and convince him to take the blame, the lawyer walked up to the other driver and said, "You are in serious trouble. I'm a lawyer!"

The driver stepped out of the car and looked the lawyer in the eye. "No, it seems you are the one in trouble here. I'm a judge."

Lawyer: Doctor, as a result of your examination, is the young lady pregnant?

Witness: The young lady is pregnant, but not as a result of my examination.

Two lawyers were hunting in a field when they came upon a couple of tracks. After examining the tracks closely, they began to argue over what kind of tracks they were. One lawyer thought they were deer tracks, while the other lawyer argued that they were elk tracks.

They were still arguing when the train hit them.

A lawyer's wife was posing nude in front of the mirror when her husband passed by. "I was at my gynecologist's office today," she bragged, "and he said I have the breasts of a 30 year old woman."

"Yeah?" the lawyer replied. "And what did he say about your ass?"

"Oh, your name didn't even come up."

Stupid Lawyers

A lawyer walked into Victoria's Secret to purchase sheer lingerie for his wife. He was shown several choices, ranging in price from $150 to $700—the more sheer the fabric, the higher the price.

The lawyer picked the one that was the most sheer, paid the $700, and took it home to his wife. After she opened the present, he asked her to go up stairs and model it for him.

The wife went upstairs, and as she was looking at the lingerie, she had an idea. "This lingerie is so sheer, it might as well be nothing. I'll just walk out naked pretending to wear it, then tomorrow I'll take it back to the store and get the $700 refund so I can buy something I actually want."

The wife appeared at the top of the staircase, and struck a pose. The lawyer looked up at her, and then frowned and said, "Well hell, for $700 you'd think they'd at least iron it."

Lawyers Joke About Everyone Else

The Texas oilman went to see his lawyer about a divorce. "I need you to get me a divorce, and pronto! That woman of mine won't act right, she won't do what I say, and I ain't gonna put up with it!"

"Well, you know, your wife is not property," the lawyer replied. "You don't own her the way you own an oil well."

"That may be true," the oilman conceded, "but at least I should have exclusive drilling rights."

"You've been brought here for stealing," the judge said to the defendant.

"Sounds great, your honor," the defendant replied. "What are we stealing and where are we getting it?"

A minister was called to testify as a witness in a slander trial. The lawyer asked the minister to repeat the slanderous statements he heard, exactly as he heard them.

"I can't do that," the minister replied. "Such words are not fit for any respectable person to hear."

"That's okay, sir," the attorney said. "Just whisper them to the judge."

Tom and John were arguing over whether Tom should file for divorce. "You can't split up over something so trivial as a weekend out with the boys," John said. "That would be stupid."

"I don't care what you say, John," replied Tom. "I just don't think she should go."

Lawyers Joke About Everyone Else

A lawyer was pulled over by a state trooper for speeding. The trooper lectured the lawyer about speeding, and did everything he could to belittle the lawyer for his driving. Finally, the trooper got around to writing the ticket. As he was filling out the forms, the trooper kept swatting at some flies that were buzzing around his head.

The lawyer said, "Looks like you are really getting bothered by those circle flies."

The trooper looked up from writing the ticket and said, "Well, I guess so, if that is what they are called. I never heard of circle flies, though. What are they?"

The lawyer replied, "Well, circle flies are common on ranches. They're called circle flies because they're almost always found circling around the back end of a horse."

The trooper said, "Oh, I see," and went back to writing the ticket, but a moment later he stopped again and asked, "Hey, are you trying to call me a horse's ass?"

The lawyer quickly replied, "Oh no, Trooper. I have too much respect for law enforcement to even think about calling you a horse's ass."

The trooper said, "Well that's a good thing," and went back to writing the ticket.

After a long pause, the lawyer said, "Hard to fool them flies though."

Q: What is the one thing dumber than a lawyer?

A: The defendant who goes to court without him.

A good friend will help you move. A great friend will help you move a dead body.

A man was forced to take a day off from work to appear for a minor traffic summons. He grew increasingly restless as he waited hour after endless hour for his case to be heard. When his name was called late in the afternoon, he stood before the judge, only to hear that court would be adjourned for the day and he would have to return the next day. "Why!!?" he snapped at the judge. Her honor, equally irked by a tedious day, roared, "That word just cost you one hundred dollars for contempt of court, that's why!" Then, noticing the man checking his wallet, the judge relented. "That's all right. You don't have to pay now." The man replied, "It's okay, I'm just seeing if I have enough for two more words."

Q: Why is a jury trial so difficult to predict?

A: The decision will be made by twelve people who weren't smart enough to get out of jury duty.

At the conclusion of the divorce trial, the judge was announcing his ruling to the parties. "Mr. Nivens," the judge said, "I've decided to give your wife $1000 per month."

"Thank you judge, that's very fair," Mr. Nivens replied. "And every once in a while, I'll try to give her a little money myself."

The lawyer was questioning the witness before the jury. "Miss Sloan," he said, "you were having an intimate relationship with Mr. Barrow, correct?"

Miss Watson replied, "Oh, no sir, we were not intimate. We were just having sex."

Q: What is the definition of alimony?

A: The screwing you get for the screwing you got.

The attorney was reviewing the facts with the defendant, and asked him, "Where were you between 6 and 8?"

The defendant thought for a moment, then replied, "Well, I'm pretty sure I was in first grade."

A man on trial for murder decides to bribe a juror so he can escape the death penalty. He tells a blonde on the jury that he will pay her $10,000 if she convinces the rest of the jury to only convict him of manslaughter. She agrees.

A few days later the jury convicts the man of manslaughter, and he is taken to jail. From the jail, he calls the blonde juror on the phone and says, "Thanks so much for saving me! I can't tell you how grateful I am."

"No problem," the blonde replies, "but it wasn't easy. Everyone else wanted to acquit you."

Q: What is the difference between a lawyer and a wife?

A: Lawyers suck.

The senior partner in the law firm told his new law clerk that his job duties included handling the partner's personal errands and tasks. His first assignment was to go to the partner's house that weekend and paint the partner's porch while he was out of town.

That Saturday, as he was driving to the partner's house, the law clerk spotted a beggar on the side of the road holding a sign, "Will Work For Food." Thinking that this would be an easy way to get the work done without having to do the labor himself, he picked up the beggar and drove him to the lawyer's house.

Once at the house, the law clerk handed the beggar the paint brush and the can of paint. "Take this stuff, go around back, and paint the porch," the law clerk told him. "If you need me, I'll be inside watching the game."

An hour later, the beggar rang the front doorbell to let the law clerk know he had finished the job.

"That was fast," the law clerk said.

"Well, it wasn't very big, so it didn't take long," the beggar replied. "But it's not a Porsche, it's a Mercedes."

A lawyer was confused about paying an invoice, so he decided to ask his secretary for some mathematical help. He called her into his office and said, "If I were to give you $20,000.00 minus 14%, how much would you take off?"

The secretary thought for a moment, then replied, "Everything but my earrings."

A man went into a lawyer's office and said, "I heard people have sued the tobacco companies for giving them lung cancer, and McDonald's for making them fat."

The lawyer said, "Yes, that's true."

The man said, "Well, I'm interested in suing too."

The lawyer said, "Okay, which one? McDonald's, or the tobacco companies?"

The man said, "Neither. I want to sue Budweiser for all the ugly people I've slept with."

The client sat down in his lawyer's office, and declared, "I want a divorce!"

"But you were just married last week," the lawyer replied. "What happened?"

"After the honeymoon," the man said, "my wife told me I'm a lousy lover."

"I can understand why you are upset, " the lawyer said, "but do you really want to divorce her just over that?"

"No," the client answered, "I want to divorce her because she knows the difference."

One mugger ran up to the other mugger. The mugger's clothes were torn, he had bruises all over his face, and he was completely out of breath. "What in the world happened to you?" the first mugger asked.

"I tried to mug this guy coming out of the bar, and he turned out to be a lawyer."

The first mugger asked, "So how much did he take from you?"

Legalese

Q: What do you get when you cross the Godfather with a lawyer?

A: An offer you can't understand.

A lawyer was pulled over by a police officer for not coming to a complete stop at a stop sign. The officer explained this to the lawyer, and asked to see his drivers license. Rather than be polite and cooperative, the lawyer decided to argue over the ticket.

"Officer, you shouldn't write me a ticket, I slowed down almost to a stop, looked both ways, and carefully drove through the intersection."

"True," the officer replied, "but you didn't come to a complete stop."

"But what the hell is the difference?" the lawyer argued again. "Slowing down is the same thing as a stop."

"I'll tell you what," the officer said. "Why don't you step out of the car and I'll explain it to you."

The lawyer got out of the car, and suddenly the police officer began beating him with his nightstick. As he struck the lawyer the fifth or sixth time, the officer asked the lawyer, "Now, do you want me to stop, or just slow down?"

Q: What do you have at the end of sex with a lawyer?

A: A boregasm.

Legalese

TOP TEN THINGS THAT SOUND DIRTY, BUT IN A LAW FIRM AREN'T:

10. Have you looked in her briefs?
9. He is one hard judge.
8. Counselor, let's do it in chambers.
7. He withdrew at the last minute.
6. Is it a penal offense?
5. Better leave the handcuffs on.
4. For $200 an hour, she better be good!
3. Can you get him to drop his suit?
2. The judge gave her the stiffest one he could.

And the number 1 thing that sounds dirty but in law isn't:

1. Think you can get me off?

The professor of a contract law class asked one of his students, "If you were to give someone an orange, what would you say?"

The student replied, "Well, okay, here's an orange."

The professor was outraged. "No! No! Think like a lawyer!"

The student paused for a minute, then replied, "Okay. I'd tell him `I hereby give and convey to you all and singular, my estate and interests, rights, claim, title, and advantages of and in, said orange, together with all its rind, juice, pulp, and seeds, and all rights and advantages with full power to bite, cut, freeze and otherwise eat, the same, or give the same away with and without the pulp, juice, rind and seeds, anything herein before or hereinafter or in any deed, or deeds, instruments of whatever nature or kind whatsoever to the contrary in anywise notwithstanding.'"

Q: What is the definition of saturated fat?

A: A lawyer in a hot tub.

When the man in the street says: "If it ain't broke, don't fix it," the lawyer writes: "Insofar as manifestations of functional deficiencies are agreed by any and all concerned parties to be imperceivable, and are so stipulated, it is incumbent upon said heretofore mentioned parties to exercise the deferment of otherwise pertinent maintenance procedures."

Q: How does a lawyer say "screw you?"

A: "Trust me."

Q: What is the definition of "court?"

A: A place where they dispense with justice.

Two law students went to the movie theatre to watch the latest blockbuster film. As actress Angelina Jolie appeared on the screen, the first law student nudged the second one and bragged, "You may find this hard to believe, but I've had her."

A few minutes later, Katie Holmes was on the screen. Again, the first law student leaned over to the second one and said, "I've had her too."

When Sienna Miller appeared on screen, the second law student leaned over to the first and said, "I suppose you're going to tell me you've had her too."

"Shhh," the first law student demanded, "I'm having her right now."

Quotable Quotes About Lawyers

Only lawyers and mental defectives are automatically exempt from jury duty.

— *George Bernard Shaw*

If there were no bad people, there would be no good lawyers.

— *Charles Dickens*

The difficult task, after one learns how to think like a lawyer, is relearning how to write like a human being.

— *Floyd Abrams*

It will be of little avail to the people that the laws are made by men of their own choice if the laws be so voluminous that they cannot be read, or so incoherent that they cannot be understood.

— *Alexander Hamilton*

A lawyer is a learned gentleman who rescues your estate from your enemies and keeps it for himself.

— *Henry Bougham*

The minute you read something you don't understand, you can be almost sure it was drawn up by a lawyer.

— *Will Rogers*

A jury consists of twelve people chosen to decide who has a better lawyer.

— *Robert Frost*

Make crime pay. Become a lawyer.

— *Will Rogers*

Any society that needs disclaimers has too many lawyers.

— *Erik Pepke*

A lawyer is never entirely comfortable with a friendly divorce, any more than a good mortician wants to finish the job and then have the patient sit up on the table.

— *Jean Kerr*

The truly successful lawyer owns his own ambulance.

— *Henny Youngman*

If I had but one life to give for my country, it would be a lawyer's.

— *Author Unknown*

Your lawyer in practice spends a considerable part of his life in doing distasteful things for disagreeable people who must be satisfied against an impossible time limit in which there are hourly interruptions from other disagreeable people who want to derail the train; and for his blood, sweat, and tears, he receives in the end a few unkind words to the effect that it might have been done better, and a protest at the size of the fee.

— *William L. Prossner*

About The Author

William L. Pfeifer, Jr., is a partner in the law firm of Pfeifer, Rose & Kolb, P.C., as well as a freelance writer. He has published articles in professional journals, newsletters, and newspapers, and is the author of *How To Start A Successful Law Practice: A New Lawyer's Guide To Opening An Office As A Solo Or Small Firm Attorney.*

Printed in the United States
129055LV00001B/100/A

9 780978 727772